The Ultimate Sales Messaging System

The 6-Step System to Clarify Your
Sales Message or Presentation

Brian Williams

ISBN: 1546931066
ISBN-13: 978-1546931065

THIS BOOK IS DEDICATED TO

The people who don't believe they are good communicators and to those who list public speaking as their #1 fear.

It's time for a new perspective.

CONTENTS

ACKNOWLEDGMENTS

I want to thank my Creator for giving me the idea for this system and the gift of communication. Without Him, I could do nothing.

Thank you, Tasha, for always believing in me.

My Why

This book could not have been written without the experience I gained over the course of my 20 years in corporate America and the clients who entrusted me with improving their advanced communication skills.

It has been a privilege to combine my love of public speaking, with the analytical skills I used as an engineer, to create a six-step system that will help presenters communicate their sales messages or presentations in a clear, concise, and compelling way.

Originally, I thought my systematic approach would be solely for those in technical sales, but I quickly realized that everyone needs advanced communication skills because, whether we like it or not, we are all in sales. We are constantly trying to sell our ideas, products, services, or talents to someone, either personally or professionally, so it was important that I develop a system that would help all presenters find success.

With *The Ultimate Sales Messaging System* I reached my goal of designing a communication system that is straightforward and easy to use. It's comprised of six simple steps that are as repeatable as the ABC's and XYZ's, and it works for everyone, regardless of their industry. I have used it across professions and have seen those who consistently use its tools, achieve increased results.

Personally, I tripled my income using this system and many of my clients have also experienced tremendous results as they have used its tools to take their advanced communication skills from mediocre to exceptional.

The Ultimate Sales Messaging System

Introduction

"No, that is not how that product works. Let me explain it one more time..." Unfortunately, that was a familiar conversation between the sales representatives and myself. I was working in a Fortune 500 as a global director of technical marketing and my job was to manage a global sales team who would meet with customers and bring their requirements back for review. I would then say yes to everything that was possible and no to everything that was not.

While I enjoyed my job, I found myself becoming more frustrated with spending so much time explaining why the product could not do what the customer was requesting. This disconnect was puzzling to me. As technical professionals - engineers and technical sales representatives, our general product knowledge was about the same, but for some reason the sales people were having a difficult time effectively communicating the capabilities of our products to potential customers. They were consistently missing sales opportunities and that was a red flag, not only to me, but also to our company executives.

It was clear that the sales representatives were not ignorant of our products, yet they were having challenges getting the customer to feel confident in our ability to provide a comprehensive solution. And although they followed the traditional sales techniques of sharing the features and benefits of our products, along with communicating our superiority over the competition, they were still losing too many sales opportunities. That is when I determined to find a solution.

I began looking at our sales presentations and asking for customer feedback when we failed to close a deal. The results were astounding. I realized the presentations they were using did not clearly and concisely address the customer's questions of how our product would make them more money or help get rid of their biggest problem. This seemed like Sales 101, so how could we miss giving the two most critical pieces of data that a customer would need to make a confident and informed buying decision? The answer was still unclear to me, so I continued my research.

Eventually, something became crystal clear. Customers did not want wordy presentations; they wanted solutions they could believe in and a clear vision for how they would get a return on their investment. They wanted sales representatives who had enough product knowledge to answer their questions, while also making the material easy to understand. Unfortunately, for our sales representatives, this was a concept they were struggling with. They were just too wordy and too technical.

As the expert, you are in a unique position because you have intimate knowledge of how your product or service works and you know if it can provide the solution your customer is looking for. However, like others before you, you may find it challenging to translate that knowledge into a message that customers can easily understand. So while the data and facts may seem clear and obvious to you, your greatest responsibility is to help your customer make an informed buying decision by effectively communicating your product knowledge without appearing condescending or overwhelming them with technical data they may not want or need.

I had to master these skills myself after leaving a 20-year corporate career to start my own communications company. I was an engineer with a new mission to develop a systematic way for sales professionals to design and deliver effective communication. I wanted it to be easy to use and simple to remember, and I got that with my systematic approach, *The Ultimate Sales Messaging System*. This system has been proven to work, not only for me, but also for the many clients who have hired my company to teach their staff the skills of exceptional communication.

I say exceptional because becoming an effective communicator is more than learning to project your voice and to make eye contact. Those things are certainly important delivery techniques, but they don't adequately address the audience's need for clear and concise sales messages and presentations. That quality of messaging doesn't come easily but is possible to achieve when we use the techniques of meticulous design and disciplined delivery.

That's what I teach in *The Ultimate Sales Messaging System*. Meticulous design and disciplined delivery tools that are used to create effective sales messages and presentations. I built my systematic approach upon three fundamentals:

1. An in depth understanding of your audience before you ever write a word on the screen.

2. A basic understanding of neuroscience and the Adult Learning Principles. Science has shown that if you understand how people think and process information, you have a better chance of successfully communicating your sales message.

3. The discipline required to design sales messages and presentations that clearly and concisely address the objectives of the audience.

When you learn to master this systematic approach to exceptional communication, you will gain:

1. **Knowledge** - To systematically design and deliver effective and exceptional communication.

2. **Commitment** - To filter your data and only present information the audience needs to know to make an informed buying decision.

3. **Growth** – You will see increased opportunities when you clearly communicate the audience's return on investment.

Remember, confused prospects rarely buy, so the more clarity you can provide, the easier it is for them to listen to your messaging and make a confident buying decision.

It's Time for a New Perspective

I have learned that exceptional communication is not obtained by doing what you have always done. You must be open to new ideas that give you a fresh perspective on what it means to design and deliver effective communication. So with that, let's start with the art and science of communication.

The Art and Science of Communication

Art

People are surprised when I talk about the *art of communication.* They don't understand what art has to do with designing effective sales messages and presentations. But every well-designed message should have an artistic expression that takes your messaging from expected to exceptional.

Art, in this context, is the creative use of images, vocal variety, humor, storytelling, word choice, graphics, data, and illustrations to create an artistic expression of a thought or an idea. Art is what makes the idea come alive. It adds flavor to the message and makes it more desirable for your audience. Remove the artistic elements, and your message is just a bland meal that no one wants to consume.

Where Has the Art Gone?

Unfortunately, many of you fall into the trap of not adding artistic elements because it's easier, safer, and more comfortable not to do so. You may even be afraid of what people will think if you break traditional presentation protocol. I understand your dilemma, that's why I'm offering you a new perspective. If you neglect to add artistic elements to your sales message or presentation, you will be guilty of lecturing, and consequently, you may fail to make an emotional connection with the audience.

When you invoke an emotional connection your message becomes memorable, and that's an important key to effective communication. With *The Ultimate Sales Messaging System,* you will learn to design exceptional communication that uses both art and science to create messaging that emotionally connects with your audience and gives them the answers they need to make an informed buying decision.

Science

Why do people dislike listening to most sales messages? Why do presenters talk too much? Why do people fail to buy your product or service? This is where understanding the science matters. If you talk too much or give too much information at one time, science has shown that your audience will be too overwhelmed to make an informed buying decision. Consequently, it's imperative that you understand the problems that are inherent in most sales messages and presentations and that you understand why these problems exist. If you do, you will learn how to avoid making these same mistakes when designing your own messaging.

Scientifically, you need to keep it short and simple, so it's wise to model exceptional communicators who design their messaging using *The Three C's of Effective Communication.*

The Three C's of Effective Communication

This communication principle has only one goal. To make sure your messaging is clear, concise, and compelling.

1. Clear – Your points must be organized

If your message is not designed in an organized manner or is full of technical jargon, complex graphs, confusing concepts, or difficult words and figures, **you will lose the attention of your audience.**

2. Concise – Your points must be short

If you have too much information in your sales message, the human brain will become overwhelmed, and consequently, **you will lose the attention of your audience**.

3. Compelling – Your points must make an emotional connection

If you don't use the Adult Learning Principles in the design of your sales message or presentation, you may fail to engage the mind of your audience and not make an emotional connection; consequently, **you will lose the attention of your audience**.

Do you see the pattern? Your sales message or presentation should always be about your audience and how they learn, understand, and process information. If you aren't considering these things when designing your messaging, you might lose the attention of your audience, and possibly, a great sales opportunity. Exceptional communicators are always aware of this challenge, so they constantly work to ensure their messaging is clear, concise, and compelling.

They know that effective communication isn't born out of the common practice of disseminating information but it occurs when you transfer ideas in a way that makes the audience believe and take action. So if your communication doesn't follow the principle of being clear, concise, and compelling, your audience could easily misunderstand your sales message or presentation, and as a result, you could easily lose opportunities.

A Change of Perspective

Often, when I ask people why they struggle with sharing their sales message or presentation, I hear the following perspectives:

1. Some people just have "it," but I don't.

2. I'm good, but I don't think I can be a great communicator.

3. I failed the last time I presented...and I might fail again.

4. My message must be perfect!

5. I am terrified! There is no way I can do this.

These are common perspectives I hear all the time, but I like to think of them as myths since they are only your truth until you learn new skills and determine to change your belief system.

The systematic approach used in *The Ultimate Sales Messaging System* was created to help you consistently design and deliver exceptional communication. And when its steps are closely followed, it will help you confidently produce communication that meets the criteria of *The Three C's of Effective Communication: Clear, Concise, and Compelling* – every time.

Now, let me crush these myths that often keep people from becoming an exceptional communicator:

1. Some people just have "it," but I don't.
Of course, there will always be people with a natural ability for *delivering* effective communication. For them, it's a skill that doesn't need to be taught, it's innate; however, even the best communicator needs to learn the

skill of *designing* exceptional communication. That ability only comes with proper preparation.

Confucius, a famous Chinese philosopher, said, "Success depends upon previous preparation, and without such preparation there is sure to be failure."

Proper preparation is the distinguishing factor that sets the exceptional communicator apart from the mediocre one. With this system, you will learn to properly design your communication and leave mediocrity behind.

2. <u>I'm good, but I don't think I can be a great communicator.</u>

The human brain is a scientific wonder that can continually change and reorganize itself. In his fascinating book, *The Brain that Changes Itself*, Norman Doidge explains the neuroscience behind the brain principle of neuroplasticity.

> **Neuroplasticity:** This is the brain's potential to reorganize by creating new neural pathways to make adaptations as it needs to.

Basically, think of the neurological changes being made in the brain as the brain's way of tuning itself to meet your needs.

This is a revolutionary scientific discovery because it means your brain is not hardwired like a computer, but rather it can learn skills not previously known and eventually overcome limitations that scientists once thought were impossible to conquer.

So with the support of brain science, I will teach you the steps to overcome your fear of inadequacy when you design and deliver your messaging. Confident preparation will allow you to move from a good communicator to a great one.

3. I failed the last time I presented...and I might fail again.

Failure is always an option, but it isn't something you have to take on as your method of operation when it comes to presenting. Realistically, even the most talented people will fail sometimes; however, they will refuse to accept failure as a limitation, instead they will use it as a catalyst to take them to the next level.

Take Michael Jordan for example. He was one of the greatest basketball players of all time but he said, "I have failed over and over again in my life and that is why I succeed." Michael Jordan did not allow failure to become his method of operation. He used it as motivation to try again, practice harder, and be more committed. Ultimately, he never gave up.

That's what I will encourage you to do on your journey to becoming an exceptional communicator - try again, practice harder, be more committed, and never give up. *The Ultimate Sales Messaging System* will give you the design and delivery tools you need to confidently overcome any failure you may have experienced in the past.

4. My message must be perfect!

Let me release you from that pressure...perfection is impossible, so stop beating yourself up with that over-inflated expectation. You may never be perfect at anything, but you can certainly learn to be exceptional.

What I want you to realize is that the typical audience is not looking for perfection. They are looking for you to be real while being informative. If you strive to be real when adding in your artistic elements - sharing ideas and stories that your audience can believe in, understand, and appreciate, you will be one step closer to becoming an exceptional communicator.

5. I am terrified! There is no way I can do this.

In my research, I found that public speaking is the most feared thing in the human psyche...more feared than death! So fear is real. It can be a defeating factor if you allow it to take over any area of your life. However, exceptional communicators will acknowledge this fear and choose not to be controlled by it. They will learn and practice new communication skills and wholeheartedly commit to designing and delivering messaging that follows the adult learning principles.

When a message is well designed, and the delivery techniques have been followed, your fear will be greatly reduced because you will be more confident in the effectiveness of your message. So with proper effort, your fear of perfection can be conquered and it will be possible for you to become an exceptional communicator who designs and delivers effective messaging that your audience can understand and appreciate.

"Everyone focuses on the presentation, but the main goal is communication. Stop presenting and begin effectively communicating your ideas to your audience."

It's all about effective communication.

Chapter 1

The Difficulty of the Problem

Communication experts often teach the importance of speaking clearly, looking the audience in the eye, moving your focus around the room, limiting hand gestures, and smiling often. Those are all good delivery techniques. But none of those techniques address the need for designing messaging that is clear, concise, and compelling.

Through personal experience, I have learned the importance of using a systematic approach when designing messages that will specifically appeal to an audience; and though I've had much success using this technique, convincing other communicators that systematic design works can be challenging. It's not that systematic design itself is difficult, but traditionally, people have been taught communication skills the same way for a very long time. People don't realize there is a more effective way. That's why I have made it my mission to break through the cog of tradition to give you a new perspective, one that makes you an architect of your sales message or presentation.

In architectural design, there is important information that has to be gathered when building a new structure. There are preliminary plans, site inspections, blueprints, construction plans, and revisions that have to take place. And while they may have different names, the same architectural principles are used in the design phase of *The Ultimate Sales Messaging System*. This phase of the system is called *The ABC's of Communication Design*.

Architectural Design vs. The ABC's of Communication Design

First and foremost, it is extremely important that you see yourself as an architect of your communication, so let's compare the principles of architectural design with *The ABC's of Communication Design* you will learn in *The Ultimate Sales Messaging System.*

1. Preliminary Plans

Architectural Design: These are used to discuss the client's overall purpose for the structure, the type of structure, and their budget.

ABC's of Communication Design: I call this *The Audience Profile.*

2. Site Inspection

Architectural Design: An architect performs a site inspection and then considers what design the building should have in relation to the site.

ABC's of Communication Design: I call this the *Basic Building Block.*

3. Blueprints

Architectural Design: The first drawings suggest the general shape and appearance of the structure, the method of construction, where it will be placed on the site, and how the inside will look.

ABC's of Communication Design: I call this *The Content Storyboard.*

4. Construction Plan

Architectural Design: The structure will be built using the plans, site inspection, and blueprints.

ABC's of Communication Design: This is where you do your *writing.*

5. Revisions

Architectural Design: The architect might have to revise the plans to meet the client's expectations.

ABC's of Communication Design: This is where you do your *editing.*

The Importance of Design

"Design works if it is authentic, inspired, and has a clear point of view. It cannot be a collection of input."

-Ron Johnson, Apple executive

Ron Johnson had it right. Design only works if it is authentic, inspired, and has a clear point of view. That's how you become an architect of your communication; you must have intense focus and disciplined design as your uncompromising standards when building your messaging. If you do this, you will stand out above the rest because most communicators don't see themselves as an architect. So rather than having a well thought out design for their communication, they fall into the typical trap of opening a software application, choosing a template, and filling in the text boxes with everything they know. I call this data dumping.

And while data dumping is often the fundamental design issue I see in sales messages or presentations, it's not the only problem communicators struggle with when designing their messaging.

Common Design Difficulties

DIFFICULTY #1: Going to the computer first.

In this modern era, it's easy to go to your computer first when creating a sales message or presentation because you probably have a plethora of templates you can choose from to make your design process faster. And while technology is smart to use, you have to be careful not to lose your authenticity by becoming dependent upon the creativity of the software and limiting yourself to the text boxes provided.

DIFFICULTY #2: Not listening to your audience.

Listening carefully is the key to inspiration, but it's a skill that is often overlooked when designing sales messages or presentations. When you design messaging that's based on your past experience, rather than listening with a fresh perspective to your audience's greatest concerns, you lose the ability to create a customized message that will clearly meet the needs of your audience.

DIFFICULTY #3: Sharing everything you know.

As an intelligent professional, you may face the common challenge of sharing everything you know about a product or service. It's not because you just like to talk, but the data matters to you, so the analytical part of your brain believes it will matter to everyone else too. However, that is not always the case, so you must be wise about how much you share and to whom you share it with.

An overwhelmed prospect is a confused prospect, and confused prospects rarely buy, so being clear and concise is imperative if you want to give your audience the information they need to make an informed buying decision.

DIFFICULTY #4: Lack of clarity

Using the collective intelligence of a team to design a solution can give you a powerful advantage; however, you have to be selective in how much you decide to put into your sales message or presentation. Every idea is not weighted equally.

If a point does not drive your audience to a buying decision or to greater belief in your product or service, then that piece of information may not belong in your message. It takes great discipline to put only the clearest ideas in your messaging but it's a fundamental step in designing exceptional communication.

Look at the picture below. What do you see?

Perhaps you saw six doors or three open laptop computers. Or maybe you saw three blocks stacked on top of one another or arrows pointing in one direction. Regardless of what you saw, you probably identified at least one thing differently than someone else. Unfortunately, that's the greatest challenge of perspective.

People can look at the same image or hear the same presentation but get completely different messages. We call this phenomenon, mutual mystification because it leads every listener to a different outcome. The result is mutual confusion, and unfortunately, it's a very common design problem.

Honing in on the perspective of every individual in your audience is difficult to do; however, mutual mystification can be significantly reduced when you learn to design sales messages or presentations that send one message to all that are listening. The tools that will help you learn to do this are covered in great detail in the chapters for *The ABC's of Communication Design*.

I am certain if I can change your perspective in this area, I can change your behavior. And if I can change your behavior, I can dramatically change your results!

Chapter 2

The Source of the Solution

In my research, I have found that the audience is the most overlooked person in a sales message or presentation. It's almost as if they are an afterthought. Typically, presenters may share everything they know about a product or service but fail miserably when it comes to intentionally addressing the issues or objectives of the audience. Unfortunately, this is a common problem, but there is a solution; it comes from understanding the Adult Learning Principles.

A Key to Success: Understanding the
Adult Learning Principles

Over the past few decades neuroscience has reached new levels of understanding about the brain and how humans best process information. And while you may think that sharing an abundance of facts will appropriately inform the audience, you are actually doing the antithesis. Unknowingly, you're overwhelming them with too much information.

Our short-term memories are designed to handle about seven, small chunks of information at a time before getting overwhelmed – that's why most phone numbers are only seven digits long. Simply put, our brains don't like working too hard to remember large amounts of information all at once, so it's very important that you understand how to use the Adult Learning Principles when designing your sales messages and presentations. These principles will allow you to successfully design messaging that appeals to the human brain and how it processes information.

Below is the Adult Learning Pyramid, which shows the different styles of learning and how much our brains tend to remember with each method. As you can see, the human brain prefers certain methods of learning to others. While you may spend most of your time lecturing, that is considered passive engagement and it is where the human brain processes the least amount of information. Instead, for maximum impact, you should try to spend most of your time engaging your audience in active learning.

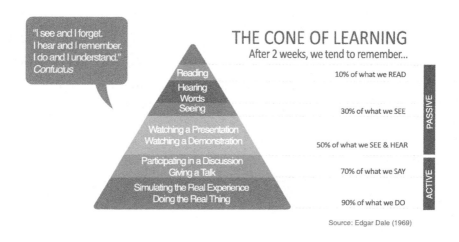

Source: Edgar Dale (1969)

The Ultimate Sales Messaging System was designed to take advantage of the brain's peak processing power by using the active learning principles of *Say and Do*. If you create sales messages and presentations that allow your audience to be active participants, rather than just reading or listening passively, you will be amazed at how often they believe, buy, and bite.

To Believe, Buy, and Bite

This is a concept I developed to describe the process of audience engagement. Engagement is the key word. You must intensely focus on capturing the attention of your audience if you want to reach the ultimate outcome of convincing them to believe, buy, and bite.

1. Believe:

This is where you design and deliver sales messages and presentations that are clear, concise, and compelling enough to make an audience believe in you and in your product or service. This is where rapport and trust are born between yourself and the audience.

The more authentic your message, the more confidence the audience will have in your knowledge and in your ability to follow through with your proposed solutions.

2. Buy:

You must be sure to create a sales message or presentation that is clear, concise, and compelling. It has to make sense to the audience, and by the end, it should give them enough information to make an informed buying decision. If your audience believes in you, and trusts that your solution will resolve their issue or concern, they will be more likely to buy your product or service.

3. Bite:

When your sales messages and presentations are clear, concise, and compelling enough to encourage your audience to buy, they will become your best marketing campaign because they have been fully convinced of the value of your product or service. Then when they express their conviction about you or your product or service, others will naturally be compelled to bite and find out more about you or your product or service too!

A New Concept That Brings Results

In our cloud-based course, *Sales Messaging University*,* we use interactive exercises to show you the negative impact of passive learning. Through your own active participation, you'll see how quickly your short-term memory is overwhelmed when you're given too much information. Our goal with this exercise is to make you sensitive to the burden you put on your audience when you overwhelm them with facts and data.

Conversely, when you allow the audience to engage with you by using the active learning principles of *Say and Do*, your message is more likely to be remembered, and subsequently, acted upon.

Engage your audience. That's one of the ways you set yourself apart as an exceptional communicator.

*http://bit.ly/SalesMsg

Chapter 3

You Talk Too Much!

"The less you talk, the more you're listened to."
-Abigail Van Buren

The Information Age has made the problem of talking too much worse than any time in modern history. With access to the Internet, we have information available to us with the click of a button. So we should not be surprised that giving too much information (TMI) is a problem that commonly appears in corporate communication, sales messages, and presentations.

Consider this: If you were hosting a wine tasting event and your guests asked for one glass of vintage red wine, you would only give them what they asked for, you would not give them the entire vineyard. Well, this same principle applies to your messaging. You need to give your audience exactly what they are looking for, and nothing more. Otherwise, you will overwhelm and frustrate them, even though that wasn't your intent.

When you give your audience only what they asked for you're using the process of filtration and the power of self-control. You need both to ensure you avoid the frustration that will naturally occur if you overwhelm your audience with information or too many words.

The Process of Filtration

The Process of Filtration is important because it forces you to reduce the quantity of information in your messaging by trimming away anything that isn't critical for your audience to know. This is important because our short-term memories don't have the capacity to process large quantities of information at one time; it's mentally exhausting. So filtering your message will increase the quality of learning for your audience.

As the graphic illustrates, when there is too much information given the quality of learning begins to dramatically decrease, so you must avoid giving too much information if you want your messaging to be effective.

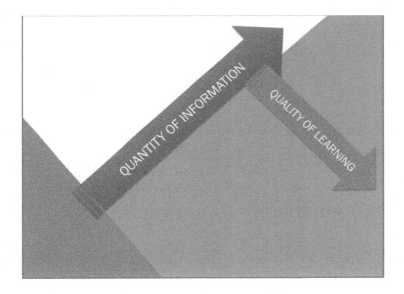

Reviewing your messaging and filtering out things that don't directly build upon your main idea may seem like a time-consuming process, but it will be a great benefit to your audience. They will have the relevant facts and details they need to make an informed buying decision and that in turn will be a great benefit to you. Conversely, if you fail to do this, you will experience what I call *filter failure* – giving an excess amount of information, and both your presentation and your audience will suffer because of it.

29

Common traps to look out for when filtering your material:

1. **Add-ons** - Adding extra facts just because you like them.
2. **Long, detailed stories** - KISS (Keep It Short Speaker).
3. **Long introductions** - Remember the value of a minute.
4. **Lack of preparation** - Use of run-ons and fill-ins, start-overs.
5. **Loving your own information** - The audience wants to know how you will solve their problem, not how much you know.

 KEY POINT: You must be relentless and filter out information that doesn't critically build upon the main idea of your message.

The Technology Trap

Daniel J. Boorstin, an American historian, said it best when he reflected on the advancement of technology. He said,

"Technology is so much fun but we can drown in our technology. The fog of information can drive out knowledge."

Don't be guilty of drowning out knowledge because you are giving too much information in your sales message or presentation. Be relentless. Filter your information and only share what is relevant to the conversation. When you do this, your audience will gain confidence in your message and in your ability to deliver your solution.

Applying a filter to your information is a key principle that is often ignored when it comes to communication. However, if you grasp this concept and begin to apply it, you will be on your way to becoming an exceptional communicator.

Apply the filter - your audience needs it.

Self-Control

Another way you unintentionally frustrate your audience is when you lack self-control in your conversation. You must be conscious of how much you're talking, because even when you're not aware of it, your audience is. Surprisingly, most presenters never realize they are overwhelming people with words and that's a huge offense. In fact, it should be a crime. I call it aggravated assault with a wordy weapon, so Keep It Short Speaker (KISS)!

Having self-control is woefully underrated but it's a powerful skill to learn if you want to become an exceptional communicator. Without it, you will certainly have problems. Your audience will experience severe boredom along with mental fatigue and they will quickly disengage. That's why you have to be disciplined and not force-feed information to your audience by talking too much.

"You need an exceptionally clear vision, something that you can say in one sentence. The fewer the words the better."

-Ron Johnson

Chapter 4

In Search of Simplicity

"Simplicity leads to clarity and clarity unleashes the true power of effective communication."

In our cloud-based course, *Sales Messaging University,** I teach you how to become an advanced communicator. I spend a great amount of time helping you understand the importance of communicating a very clear and concise message. And while that may seem obvious, employing both clarity and simplicity is typically very difficult for most presenters to do. Not because they are incapable, but traditionally, they've been taught to regurgitate the features and benefits of their products and services, so helping them see there's a better way takes time.

I want to reassure you that clarifying and simplifying your messaging comes down to one thing – filtering. You must filter your data down to the most important facts and avoid these common presentation pitfalls:

1. Cultural clichés
Clichés reflect phrases that are commonly known and are popular within a certain culture. It's best that you don't use them in your sales message or presentation because they could possibly cause confusion for those who don't understand their meaning. Here are some examples:

    a. "Don't throw the baby out with the bath water."

    b. "Pick the low hanging fruit."

*http://bit.ly/SalesMsg

c. "A slam dunk deal."

2. A meandering message

Messages that jump from topic to topic or point to point are very difficult to follow and will cause the audience to mentally disengage from your sales message or presentation. It's very difficult for your audience to mentally create structured thought from a meandering message. For example:

If a person were to begin reading a book in chapter 4, then move to chapter 1, then to chapter 11, etc. they would never have a healthy understanding of the book. So the flow of your message should be logical and sequential.

3. Aggravating acronyms

Acronyms are simply abbreviations created from the first letter of each word in a phrase or series of words. There is usually a false assumption that everyone knows what the acronyms mean. Don't underestimate the power of this bad habit. If acronyms must be used, always define them. Here are some examples:

1. AKA – Also Known As
2. OT – Overtime
3. DOB – Date Of Birth
4. MIA – Missing In Action

Never assume that everyone understands. Always clarify.

4. Cute and crazy

This is when you do something that you think is cute, but when others see it, it may seem crazy and be misunderstood. You must be careful when you add anything that might undermine your credibility or cause your audience to become uncomfortable.

The Curse of Knowledge

My grandmother would often say that some people know too much for their own good. What she meant was a person can be so confident in their knowledge of a topic that they become oblivious to what they don't know. I see this happen all the time in sales messages and presentations. The presenter is so familiar with their product or service that they forget there are terms and concepts that can be confusing to an audience; consequently, they forget to slow down or explain new ideas. Why does this happen? It's called the *Curse of Knowledge*.

In their best selling book, *Made to Stick,* Chip and Dan Heath, discuss this principle. They call it *The Curse of Knowledge.* The premise is that once you know something, you find it difficult to imagine what it was like to never know it. In essence, your knowledge has "cursed" you. Therefore, when sharing a message or presentation, be careful not to share at a level that is beyond the understanding or interest of your audience. When you do, it destroys your sales message or presentation. I know this can be challenging, but here are two solutions you can use to break the "curse":

<u>SOLUTION #1</u> - Use powerful quotes and images

Quotes from credible sources add validity, interest, and sometimes clarity to your sales message or presentation - so use them. Using powerful images at the right time can help reinforce a point more than words can. For example, throughout this book I have used several quotes and images to engage your brain rather than giving a long explanation. The use of quotes or images can be a powerful aid to providing clarity.

SOLUTION #2 - Speak in a language they already know

When you are trying to communicate a difficult or technical concept, your best approach is to use language and examples that your audience is already familiar with. Taking this approach allows the audience to easily understand the point you're trying to communicate. For example, here is a simplified explanation for 3-D printing:

> "Have you ever seen a clay model of an automobile before they build the real car? Well, 3-D printing is basically the same concept, except it uses plastic or metal to "print" or create a 3-D model of the product."

 SCIENCE FACT: "Every new idea must build on ideas that the student already knows." –Daniel Willingham

No Longer a "Curse"

Using powerful quotes and images and speaking in a language your audience already understands will take time, but if you put forth the effort, these principles will help you become an exceptional communicator. Your knowledge will no longer be a "curse" to you, but instead, it will be an asset that gives you credibility.

Remember, simplicity is not simple. It takes time.

KEY POINT: Remember to always apply the Filtration Process to your material to achieve simplicity. If it doesn't drive the audience towards the main idea of your message in some way, eliminate it!

Chapter 5

Will They Remember?

The purpose of making your messaging clear and concise is that you want your audience to remember what you told them. What good is it to share a message that everyone quickly forgets? You need your message to "stick" if you want your audience to make an informed buying decision.

 KEY POINT: To "stick" means that your ideas are understood and easily remembered; therefore, having a greater impact.

When I was creating *The Ultimate Sales Messaging System*, I learned six principles about "brain stickiness" that I want to share with you. These principles discussed in the book, *Made to Stick,* reiterate why you need to strive to create sales messages or presentations that are clear, concise, and compelling.

1. Simplicity

Less is best. Research shows the more points you have, the less you accomplish. For example:

a. If you have 3 points, your audience remembers 2-3.

b. If you have 4-9 points, they remember 1 or 2.

c. If you have 9+ points, they remember NOTHING!

 KEY POINT: The more points you have, the less they remember. Keep it simple.

2. Unexpectedness (surprise or suspense)

Your first job is to get the attention of your audience and then you must keep it. Unexpectedness guarantees an attentive audience. You cannot tell them everything; you must create mystery and suspense. In the movie industry they call it a "bathroom blocker."

A bathroom blocker is that scary or incredibly engaging action scene in a movie that "blocks" you from wanting to leave your seat to go to the bathroom. So what does that mean to you? That means you need to keep your sales messages or presentations interesting enough that your audience doesn't know what to expect next. This assures they stay engaged from the beginning to the end of your message.

 KEY POINT: You must violate the audience's expectation.

 SCIENCE FACT: Our memory gives preferential treatment to ideas or events that have a strong emotional connection.

3. Concreteness

Make the point. Avoid vague, rambling, and cute language. Use terms that people understand or define ones they may not know. Speaking concretely is the only way your audience will remember the main idea of your sales message or presentation.

Research has shown that people remember concrete ideas far better than abstract or vague ideas. For example, people have a concrete understanding of the word "bicycle," but when you say the word "justice," which is more abstract, they may understand it to mean different things.

VS.

4. Credibility

Your ideas are more "sticky" when they come from credible sources, so whether you like it or not, your audience will always consider the source. Your source does not always have to be a person. It can be statistics, hard facts and details, or an expert reference with strong credentials.

5. Emotions

In order for your audience to care about your ideas, they must feel something. The more emotions that are engaged, the more connected the audience will be to your message. When I say emotion I mean the use of compassion, energy, sadness, joy, fear, anger, and elation.

 KEY POINT: "Presentation is about the transfer of emotion." - Seth Godin

6. <u>Stories</u>

Research shows that stories connect with the brain in ways that facts, data, and statistics do not. The Harvard Business Review had a great perspective:

> "When executives need to persuade an audience, most try to build a case with facts, statistics, and some quotes from authorities. In other words, they resort to "company-speak," the tools of rhetoric they have been trained to use. Executives can engage people in a much deeper - and ultimately more convincing way, if they toss out their Power Point slides and memos and learn to tell good stories."

A Griot - A storyteller in West Africa whose function was to keep an oral history of the tribe or village. They would also entertain with stories, poems, songs, dance, etc. This historical "recording" has succeeded for millennia.

You should not downplay the practice of using good stories when communicating your sales message or presentation to your audience. The more your audience can relate to your stories, the more impactful your messaging and the greater your rapport with them.

KEY POINT: "The human mind seems exquisitely tuned to understand and remember stories. In fact, psychologists sometimes refer to stories as "psychologically privileged," meaning that they are treated differently in memory than other types of material." –Willingham

The Four C's of a Good Story

Stories sell everyday. They sell in movies, commercials, and in effective marketing materials because they connect with the heart and mind of the observer; therefore, your sales messages or presentations should tell a good story if you want to make an impactful connection with your audience. Consider The Four C's of a Good Story:

1. Causality

In causality, the events are connected to one another so they occur in sequence. Simply put, there is a cause and then an effect that happens. For example:

a. Because our sales have decreased by 18% over the last five quarters, we will have to terminate 8 employees.

b. The customer has agreed to buy more products because we delivered ahead of schedule.

When you use sequence in your stories, each point reasonably connects to the next. Random and disconnected points confuse the listener and ruin the experience of a good story.

2. Conflict

When there is conflict in stories, the main character is in pursuit of a goal, but something always lies in the way. This is where the audience becomes engaged because they are now invested in the outcome. In the same way, your sales message or presentation should always highlight the conflict so your audience is aware of your struggle to find a solution. For example:

a. While going through a potential buyout, the interim CEO decides he needs to cut overhead in some way.

b. A once successful product has lost significant market share, what will happen to the product and the production team?

3. Complications

Every good story has some type of complication. This is when challenges and difficulties arise during the pursuit of a goal. Your sales message or presentation should address any complications that might occur as you work toward presenting your solution. For example:

a. To reduce the company overhead, we need to reduce employee hours, but first, we have to meet with union representatives and get them to agree.

b. Time Cable wants to merge with Excel Entertainment but the Federal Communications Commission needs to approve the deal first.

4. Character

In a story, the character is an interesting person with unique qualities and full of action. In your sales message or presentation, the characters presented should be the ones who will help bring resolution to the conflict. For example:

a. John Clark, an industrial psychologist who once led government terrorist negotiations, will meet with the union representatives to discuss the terms of the deal.

b. Susan James, the first female producer for a prime time network, will meet the FCC to discuss the benefits of the merger between Time Cable and Excel Entertainment.

Stories engage the heart and mind so keep your audience engaged with your sales message or presentation by using stories.

Check Yourself: Do They Remember?

At the end of your sales message or presentation ask yourself two questions to determine if you have effectively communicated your message:

1. Can the audience easily repeat the main idea of your sales message or presentation?

2. Does the audience believe in your message enough to do what you have asked them to do?

If you can answer yes to these two questions, then you can be certain you effectively communicated your message in a way that is clear, concise, and compelling. Therefore, it will be remembered.

Chapter 6

Visuals
(Sometimes Referred to as Slides)

There are differing opinions about the necessity of using visuals. Personally, I think if they're used correctly, visuals can add great value to a presentation. Here are some common questions I'm often asked:

Q: Do I need to use visuals?
A: It depends on what you're presenting. Never assume that you must use visuals. They should only be used if they add real value, not decoration.

Q: When should I use visuals?
A: When you can easily replace one hundred words or excessive facts or data with an image or graphic, you should use them.

Q: What is the purpose of visuals?
A: Visuals should reduce complexity, increase understanding, and decrease the audience's short-term memory workload. If your visuals do that, you should use them.

The Four Principles of Visual Communication

A key component in helping you design communication that is clear, concise, and compelling are *The Four Principles of Visual Communication: Simplicity, elegance, focus, and clarity.*

Using these principles will help you determine if your visuals have a clearly defined purpose and will make a meaningful impact in your sales message or presentation.

1. Simplicity

Your visuals should simplify what was formerly complex. If the visual needs explanation to be understood, then it doesn't have simplicity.

2. Elegance

You should design visuals that are appealing to the eye, full of color, contrast, and spatial balance...while engaging the senses. You cannot fall into the trap of having too much happening on a visual; it will just confuse the viewer.

3. Focus

When viewing your visual, it should be clear to the audience what they should focus on and what the main message is. You can force the viewer to focus on the main objective of the visual by either highlighting the area of interest or blurring or cropping out irrelevant portions of the image.

4. Clarity

The visual should be easy to comprehend in 5 seconds or less, otherwise, it is too complex or too busy.

Drop the Crutch!

As a presenter, it's important that your slide deck doesn't become a crutch to get through your sales message or presentation. Your visuals should only enhance what you already plan to say, so they should not:

1. Be used as a guide

You are the expert in the room so you must act like it by taking the audience through your sales message or presentation with confidence. When you depend upon your slide deck to tell the story, you bore the audience, miss an opportunity to create rapport them, and lose credibility as the expert.

2. Be used as a substitute for good content

Content is king. Therefore, if your sales message or presentation is lacking quality content that answers the concerns and issues of the audience, you have failed them. Remember, your visuals should compliment your content.

3. Be loaded with text

You must remember to keep your information simple, clear, concise, and compelling. We all have seen sales messages or presentations that are heavy laden with text. You cannot be guilty of this if you want to become an exceptional communicator.

4. Be complex

As a professional, you have to be careful not to fall into the habit of relying on complex data, charts, and graphs to communicate your points. While those things may look impressive, they can become a huge distraction to your audience and cause confusion.

Remember, confused prospects rarely buy, so keep it simple.

"Communication is about getting others to adopt your point of view, to help them understand why you're excited (or sad, or optimistic, or whatever else you are). If all you want to do is create a file of facts and figures, then cancel the meeting and send in a report!" -Seth Godin

Setting Yourself Apart

If you desire to become an exceptional communicator, you set yourself apart by creating visuals for your sales message or presentation that will help your audience make an informed buying decision.

"True presentations focus on the presenter and the visionary ideas and concepts they want to communicate. The images (slides) reinforce the content visually rather than create distraction, allowing the audience to comfortably focus on both. It takes an investment of time on the part of the presenter to develop and rehearse this type of content, but the results are worth it." - Nancy Duarte

Take the time to design visually appealing content that follows *The Four Principles of Visual Communication* and you will set yourself apart as an exceptional communicator.

Chapter 7

Organizing the "Scenes"
Of Your Messaging

Another advanced technique for making your communication easy to understand and remember, is designing the structure of your sales message to flow like a good movie. I like to call this process continuity. Continuity is the art of organizing the "scenes" of your sales message or presentation into an order that promotes clear understanding for your audience.

It's very difficult to follow messaging when the structure is random and chaotic. For example, you would never know your true destination if you started at mile marker 28, ran to marker 6, then back to 52, you would be confused. However, when you have continuity in your sales message or presentation you will give your audience a structured path to follow.

Examples of Continuity

1. <u>Chronological order (messaging ordered by time)</u>
The simplest approach to communicating events in time or the steps in a process is to share how they happened or the order in which they need to happen.

2. <u>Climactic order (from least important to most important)</u>
If your message is trying to make a logical appeal, you might begin your sales message or presentation with a general statement, presenting specific details in order of increasing importance, and then ending with a dramatic

statement - a climax.

3. Problem-solution order (give the problem then a solution)

With this type of message you are trying to convince the audience to take a particular course of action. You may indicate what's wrong and then explain how to fix it.

4. Topical order (messaging ordered by topic)

This involves taking the main topic of your message and dividing it into several subtopics. The subtopics are always related to the main topic. The order of the subtopics doesn't matter.

5. Logical order (points flow naturally from one to the next)

With this approach, you develop points and order information in a way to keep the audience focused on the main idea in your sales message or presentation. It helps you design with clarity.

 KEY POINT: The path you take should be communicated very clearly to your audience. This will act as a mental GPS system that allows them to easily follow along with you.

Adding "Brain Candy" to Your Presentation

"Brain Candy" is the finishing detail that will take your sales message or presentation from mediocre to exceptional. This is where you'll organize the content of your message and make sure the messaging flows seamlessly between points. You add "brain candy" in two ways: Storyboarding and Transitions.

Storyboarding

Created in the 1930's by Walt Disney Studios, storyboarding uses a sequence of images to "preview" a movie (or any communication) before producing the final product. The storyboard acts as a fast and efficient way to edit and properly design the content. Most movies, commercials, and websites that are created today use storyboarding in their design process.

Creating the storyboard is not difficult once you have a well-designed sales message or presentation. With the help of sticky notes, you can begin to order the main points of your content in a way that will make your message clear to the audience. Using sticky notes allows you to move your content around until you find the flow that best communicates your message.

 KEY POINT: If your audience cannot track with you or follow your reasoning, you're officially wasting their time.

While it takes time to create a storyboard, putting forth the effort to write your content on paper before putting it into a software application makes it easier to see if your message is well organized.

Transitions

In your communication, a transition is the glue that holds the "scenes" of your storyboard together. Without transitions, your message will appear to meander and the audience will find it difficult to continually track with you. This is when you lose your audience to confusion and boredom. Transitions provide your audience with the mental direction they need to follow your ideas and easily understand your message.

Examples of Transitions

1. <u>Conference event at a local hotel</u>

    a. Point A - 4500 people will attend on the last day

    b. **Transition** - since next year will be even larger...

    c. Point B - the event will be at the Convention Center.

2. <u>New product release</u>

    a. Point A - We have more than 3 critical bugs

    b. **Transition** - for example...

    c. Point B - voice mail only records for 12 seconds instead of 24.

3. <u>14 year old son is going through puberty</u>

    a. Point A - My son is asking about girls and intimacy

    b. **Transition** - since, I can no longer ignore his questions...

    c. Point B - I broke down and ordered "Passport to Purity."

 KEY POINT: Transitions act as mental signposts. They allow your audience to easily follow the order of your message. Don't arrive at the conclusion without them.

Pay Attention to the Feedback

When you create a sales message or presentation you always want to pay attention to the feedback you get after its delivery to see what your audience thought of it. If your audience feedback is...

1. Your message was a bit "choppy" or "jumpy."

2. I had a hard time following you, so I jumped on Twitter.

3. I had trouble understanding how points 2 and 3 related.

4. I felt like the ideas hopped around without connecting.

5. Sorry, I cannot buy. I don't understand what you're selling.

These are signs that your message lacks continuity and may need clearer transitions. Remember, when the information presented is chaotic and random, the understanding of your audience is limited, so the use of storyboards and transitions can help you create continuity in your sales message or presentation.

Confused prospects rarely buy, so be clear.

Now that we have reviewed the importance of designing messaging that is clear, concise, and compelling, let's learn the 6-steps of *The Ultimate Sales Messaging System*.

The Ultimate Sales

Messaging System

Chapter 8

OVERVIEW:
The Ultimate Sales Messaging System

The Ultimate Sales Messaging System is broken into two sections: Design and Delivery.

DESIGN

The design section is made up of three steps, called the *ABC's of Communication Design*. This is where you will learn to design your sales messages and presentations using an *Audience Profile*, *Basic Building Block*, and *Content Storyboard*.

These tools will help you design a sales message or presentation that will drive the audience towards your expected outcome and give them the information they need to make an informed buying decision.

DELIVERY

The delivery section is made up of three steps, called the *XYZ's of Communication Delivery*, and this is where you will learn the delivery techniques of, *eXamining Your Content*, *Your Preparation*, and *Zeroing in on Your Audience*.

These tools will ensure that your sales message or presentation engages your audience and that it is clear, concise, and compelling.

Your Focus Has to Be The Audience

Throughout *The Ultimate Sales Messaging System* you will be directed to focus intensely on the audience, not solely on the content of your sales message or presentation. While the messaging is important, if it doesn't adequately address the issues or objectives of your audience, your words will mean nothing to them, and may ultimately result in a lost opportunity.

I know that staying intensely focused on the audience may require a change of perspective if you have been traditionally trained to focus on communicating the features and benefits of your products and services. It's a common practice. But in my experience, those presenters who learn to put the needs of their audience above their own knowledge and expertise are the ones who become exceptional communicators.

It's Not About You

The Ultimate Sales Messaging System is all about them, not about you, so your focus needs to be on creating sales messages or presentations that address the issues or objectives of your audience. If you do this, they will engage with you because they know you have listened well and have made their concerns your greatest focus. Not only will you increase your credibility in their eyes, but you will also make it easier for them to see the value of choosing your product or service.

The ABC's of

Communication Design

Step1:

The Audience Profile

Chapter 9

ABC's of Communication Design:
The Audience Profile

Since the audience is often the most overlooked person in the design of a sales message or presentation it's important that you learn to pay attention to them in a new way. I'm not talking about knowing the number of attendees or even their names and positions, that's a given. Instead, I'm referring to a collection of facts that are going to help you intentionally present the information your audience needs to make a clear and informed buying decision. Most presenters don't know how to do this, and if that's you, you're in good company, just not in good practice. That's why I created the *Audience Profile* to help you.

Step 1: The Audience Profile

The first step you are instructed to complete in *The Ultimate Sales Messaging System* is the creation of an *Audience Profile*. It's a living document that should be continuously updated to reflect the dynamics of the audience you are presenting to. It will help you hone in on the details that matter to your audience and keep you focused on providing the information that will help them make a clear and informed buying decision.

There are ten fundamentals that should always be included in the *Audience Profile*. They are:

1. Purpose of the Meeting

This is where you document why the meeting is being held. Having a clear understanding of why you are meeting will make it easier for you to create a sales message or presentation that is focused on addressing the issues or objectives of your audience.

2. Decision Makers

Who are the people in the room with the authority to make the buying decision? You must know whom these people are before going into a meeting.

3. Target Audience

Who are the people you would like to attend the meeting or to see your sales message or presentation? They need an invite. Write down their names and make sure you give them adequate time to commit.

4. Presentation Name

Choose a title for your sales message or presentation that clearly identifies what will be discussed. If you are vague here, you may not get the attendance response that you need and desire.

5. Meeting Location/Date/Time

This is actually a very important piece of information that is usually overlooked. Once you consider your target audience, where is the best place to meet to get the outcome you are hoping for? Your office is not always the best place, so carefully consider the attendees and decide if it would be more strategic to meet on their territory rather than on your own.

Is there an ideal date or time for the meeting attendees? Choose a date and time that makes it easy for them to attend.

6. <u>Number of Expected Attendees</u>

How many people should be expected to attend the meeting? Remember, the more attendees, the more feedback and opinions you have to consider. Strive to only invite those you know need to be at the meeting or presentation.

7. <u>Technical Content Needed</u>

Will you need technical content? If so, how technical should it be on a scale of 1-10, with 1 being minimally technical and 10 being heavily technical? As a presenter, you may like technology, data, facts, charts, and graphs but you need to be sure to choose the appropriate amount of technical content for your audience.

Confusion kills sales and opportunities.

8. <u>Expected Outcome</u>
Think:

When the meeting is over, what thoughts do you want to leave in the mind of your audience? What do you want them to think? Perhaps it's, "That company paid close attention to our Request for Proposal (RFP). They really understand our issues."

Say:

What do you want them to say when you are done? When they leave the meeting or the conference call, what do you want your audience to say to their colleagues?

Do:

Now that you know what you want them to think and what you want them to say, what is it that you want them to do when you are done?

This is important to decide before you design a message or presentation. Be specific. Maybe you want them to schedule a follow up meeting, agree to hire you, or just decide to do the deal; either way, consider in advance what you want the end result to be and design your message to get that result.

Success is not accidental. The more you focus on the desired outcome, the more likely you are to successfully achieve it.

9. Allies

List the people in the room who will most likely agree with the solution or ideas that you are presenting. These are your allies. You should make a point to speak with them before the meeting so you can get further buy-in from them. And during the sales message or presentation, if you need a confidence boost, make eye contact with them often.

Everything counts, so you will want to leverage any "friendlies" that you may have. Your goal should be to have advocates in the room that will support, encourage, and agree with your points in front of their colleagues. Identify these people in advance and make sure they can attend your meeting.

What success looks like: We recently did some work for a client in Silicon Valley and we overwhelmed them with value. Once we identified the manager's expectations, we made sure to meet and exceeded them. As a result, we created an ally that day! In fact, our ally was so confident in our ability to deliver that they easily convinced another manager to hire our company for an upcoming project.

That is why you should find or create an ally and invite them to your sales meeting or presentation. Their positive feedback and support can be your best marketing campaign.

10. Objectors

These are the people you know in advance are resistant to you, your ideas, or your solution. When considering your objectors you need to think about what might cause this group of people to give you push back. Then, address those concerns directly in your sales message or presentation in order to diffuse any tension.

Having this type of foresight, will save you unnecessary frustration and possibly keep your objectors from distracting the rest of the audience from making an informed buying decision.

Don't ignore the elephant in the room - sit on it!

The Value of this Tool

If you learn to create an *Audience Profile* before designing your sales message or presentation, you will save yourself time because you will go into the design phase with laser focus on whom you are speaking to and what you want your outcome to be. This intense focus will stop you from adding unnecessary information and better prepare you to address the issues or concerns of those who may be resistant to you, your ideas, or your solutions.

Using the *Audience Profile** keeps your focus on the most important person in the room, the audience, and it's the first step in *The Ultimate Sales Messaging System*.

*To download a free copy of the Audience Profile, go to:

http://bit.ly/AudProf

The ABC's of Communication Design

Step 2:
The Basic Building Block

Chapter 10

ABC's of Communication Design:
The Basic Building Block

In the *Basic Building Block* there is a foundational principle that you must clearly understand to design exceptional communication, it's called The Cornerstone. The cornerstone is what drives your audience to your expected outcome, so understanding how it works is extremely important.

The Cornerstone Concept

In construction, the cornerstone is the first stone set in a masonry foundation. It's of critical importance since all other stones will be set in reference to the cornerstone; consequently, the placement of this stone will determine the position of the entire structure.

This masonry concept applies well to the design of effective sales messages or presentations because your messaging also needs a strong content foundation. Similarly, your identified cornerstone will become a central piece of your communication. Without it to guide you, you may fail to design a message that is as clear and effective as you need it to be.

Building on the Cornerstone

Look at the following examples to see how the presenter will use the cornerstone to help build their sales message or presentation.

SITUATION #1: Corporate Sales

a. **Presenter** - Vice President of Sales

b. **Cornerstone** - Sales team to increase sales by 12%

Since the Vice President of Sales needs to increase sales by 12%, he or she will keep the content focused on that goal. Every example, illustration, chart, data point, or graph will be about achieving the outcome of 12% growth so the sales teams will understand clearly what needs to be done and the time frame they have to reach the goal.

SITUATION #2: Human Resource Conference

a. **Presenter** - Motivational speaker

b. **Cornerstone** - To improve morale and inspire change

The motivational speaker knows that company morale has been low, so he or she will be certain to include inspirational stories, examples, and illustrations that the audience can relate to and believe in.

The presenter will not discuss negative events or consequences but will focus on ideas or stories that encourage positive change and make the employees feel good about what they do.

SITUATION #3: Comedy Event

a. **Presenter** - Comedian

b. **Cornerstone** - To make people laugh and have a good time

The comedian understands that the audience came to have fun, so the content will be carefully chosen to be humorous and inoffensive. He or she will choose jokes that have proven to draw laughter before and that keep the audience engaged.

SITUATION #4: Faith Organization

a. **Presenter** - Pastor, Rabbi, Priest, Imam, or any spiritual leader

b. **Cornerstone** - To help people believe in God

The spiritual leader has strong faith and has a heart to help people. He or she will be certain to share their personal experiences of faith, the stories of other believers, and carefully answer questions that may hinder a person's belief in God.

SITUATION #5: Family Relationships

a. **Presenter** - Parent

b. **Cornerstone** - To teach their child important life lessons

The parent will consider the youthfulness and naivety of children and share age appropriate stories, examples, and hands-on learning experiences to train them for different lessons in their lives.

As you can see, the cornerstone is the foundational reference point for every situation. All examples, stories, or ideas were chosen to complement the cornerstone's goal of driving the audience to the expected outcome. It gives a sales message or presentation a focused foundation, so it's an essential component of the *Basic Building Block* step.

Let's explore further how you can use the cornerstone concept in your message or presentation to create a marketing masterpiece.

Creating a Masterpiece

You will create a marketing masterpiece if you can successfully tie your company's "secret sauce" to your well-defined cornerstone. Your "secret sauce" is the distinguishing factor that sets your product or service apart from your competition. It's also known as your value proposition.

When you know how you differ from your competition, and you learn to capitalize on that difference, you can create a communication strategy that will pay great returns. For example, is your company known for getting its product out in record time? Are you known for providing an exceptional customer experience or creating a unique and customized solution? No matter your area of expertise, if you learn to merge your "secret sauce" with your cornerstone, you will have the beginnings of a powerful sales message or presentation. Let's look at the following example to see how it's done.

"Secret Sauce" + The Cornerstone

Secret sauce: Fastest production times in the industry
Cornerstone: To get the client to use our production services

The Marketing Masterpiece:

"Mr. Client, you said your company goal for this year is to cut your delivery time in half from four days to two. While some people may think that's an impossible goal, we understand how this change will give you a significant advantage over your competition, and we believe we can help you.

Our company has been proven to have the fastest production times in the industry. As a result, we can get Widget A back to you within two days, though the industry standard is five. Mr. Client, if you choose to use our production services, you will have a

72 hour delivery advantage over your nearest competitor and reach your two day delivery goal. Here are the analytics to prove our ability and a few case studies to prove our success."

In this example, we first addressed the main objective of our audience - cutting their delivery times in half. Then we pointed them back to our cornerstone – hire our company for the job. When you start with the audience's greatest issue or objective, they will listen carefully because they know you're genuinely concerned with finding a solution to their problem.

Next, we addressed our cornerstone of getting the client to choose our production services. We shared that we have been proven to have the fastest production times in the industry, so with our help, they could reach their delivery goal of two days. Here we show our value proposition and why we are the company they should choose for production services.

It's unnecessary to share your entire company history. Just give your audience the pertinent information they need to make an informed buying decision. In this example, giving them our analytics and case studies to use as a reference would strengthen our credibility and offer clarity for their decision making process.

Finally, we end with reminding them that their goal will be met if they choose our solution. No hard sell, just simple facts that make it easy for the audience to determine if our services offer the best solution.

Do you see how merging the "secret sauce" together with the cornerstone makes for a powerful sales message or presentation? The marketing masterpiece that occurs when you merge together your "secret sauce" and cornerstone, will allow you to address what is most important to your audience, while at the same time, getting buy in for your cornerstone.

KEY POINT: A sales message or presentation should always have a cornerstone. This is the main idea you want your audience to walk away with. Structurally, all other points will be designed around the cornerstone.

Step 2: The Basic Building Block

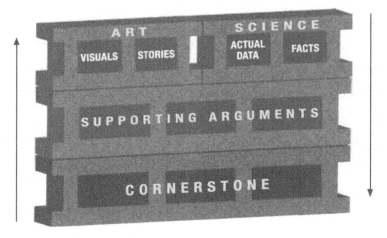

The Basic Building Blocks of Exceptional Communication™

As the diagram shows, the cornerstone is the foundation of your sales message or presentation. It's the most important idea you want to clearly communicate to your audience. Then you add your supporting arguments, art, and science to build the rest of your messaging. Use the *Basic Building Block* to make sure your sales messages and presentations are focused and have a clear cornerstone.

The Cornerstone – Where it All Begins

Again, your cornerstone is your main idea - the single main point you want to convey to your audience. As seen in the previous examples, you should write it down and make sure it is brief, focused, and can stand on its own. Don't add other thoughts or ideas to it. If you have more than 30 minutes to present, perhaps you could add a second point. Usually having a single point can help you move closer to success as it is easier for the audience to believe, buy, and bite when the cornerstone is simple and clearly defined.

Supporting Arguments

This is where you add the content that supports your well-defined cornerstone. You should have spent time carefully listening to your audience in your information gathering sessions so this isn't the place to guess what's important to them. Your supporting arguments are your opportunity to clearly address their issues or concerns; therefore, make sure the content you use here is clear, concise, and compelling.

I want to be certain that you understand this concept, so let's use the earlier scenario where the Vice President of Sales is discussing the need to increase sales by 12%.

One concern could be the sales team doesn't know how to generate new leads. So what supporting argument could the Vice President use to get to her cornerstone of increasing revenue by 12%?

She could tell them to reach out to their target market by posting articles with free and meaningful content on LinkedIn. The return on this effort may eventually generate a lead that can be converted to a sale.

The Vice President's supporting argument is driving her audience to her cornerstone. She needs a 12% increase in revenue and they need more sales, so she is giving them an idea through her supporting argument on how they can generate new leads.

If your supporting argument doesn't drive the audience toward your cornerstone that means it is driving them away from it. I call that both a distraction and a mistake.

Distractions kill sales and frustrate audiences.

Art

How you engage the mind of your audience can vary based on the art you choose to communicate with. For example, stories and images are a powerful artistic resource because they quickly engage the brain and make the information much easier to remember. If we continue with our example of the Vice President who is trying to increase revenue by 12%, we can see how art can be used in her presentation to the sales team.

After encouraging the sales team to reach out to their target market by posting articles on LinkedIn, she could use step-by-step screen shots to show how easy it is to post articles. By doing this, she gives them a visual of the process that they can follow later while also alleviating any technology concerns.

When you are sharing a new concept, especially one that requires the use of technology, try to incorporate graphics instead of long descriptions or explanations. Artistically, visuals are typically more effective and will be a helpful resource later when your audience tries to execute your solution on their own.

Here are some additional examples of artistic expression that you can use in your communication:

Songs – Either sing the song yourself or play an excerpt that powerfully conveys the point you are trying to make. You could use a clip from a music video as well.

Images – Images that include close-ups of people are always more engaging since the brain connects more strongly with the faces of others; however, there are many powerful images that don't include people that could convey your point just as well. Some online resources I like to use are BigStockPhoto.com, Shutterfly.com, or iStockPhoto.com. Occasionally, I use free images from unSplash, PicJumbo, or Pixabay.

Graphics/Illustrations – For custom designed graphics you could try GraphicRiver.net, CreativeMarket.com, or PhotoDune.net. Instead of using long flowing text, replace a thousand words with a custom designed image.

Another tool that I like to use is an Infographic. These are images or illustrations that tell a story in a graphical way. You can replace ten pages of text with a one-page Infographic that uses images more than words. If you cannot create one yourself, you can go to Fiverr.com and hire someone to create an Infographic for you. Typically, their designers can create custom images for very affordable prices.

Videos – When words cannot adequately convey your message, videos can be a powerful resource to use, as long as they are not too long or boring. Personally, I like using video. Vimeo.com is a great site to find already recorded video or you can create your own. Of course it takes more time to find the right video, but it can be well worth the effort. The more you do, that others don't, will put you further ahead of the competition.

Humor – Humor used correctly and at the right time is always appreciated. If you can handle this, go for it. If not, just leave it alone; there are plenty of other options. But if you're comfortable, humor can be a great addition to a presentation – I don't mean become a comedian, just be light-hearted and humorous at times.

Demonstrations – Demonstrations allow for audience interaction and often make a greater impact than if you were only speaking. Personally, depending on the topic and the audience, I'm a huge fan of bringing unexpected things to a presentation. I have used optical illusions, cards, cash, oversized items, video demonstrations, and animation to drive home my point. I always engage one or more audience members so they have fun, learn something, and most importantly, never forget the point I was trying to make. The key here is to never put your audience in an uncomfortable or embarrassing situation. Never.

Keep in mind that people typically receive information more readily when it's delivered in an artistic envelope, so be creative and don't hold back. If you find something that's a little out of the ordinary, and it's also audience appropriate, use it. However, when choosing your artistic expression, it's important that you don't choose things that would be considered offensive, distasteful, or rude.

Here's the point I'm trying to make: Audiences are tired of boring sales messages and presentations so generously add artistic elements.

Science

Scientific data adds a layer of credibility, so people tend to believe the content you are sharing more quickly when it's supported by facts and data.

With that said, adding scientific evidence that affirms your supporting arguments will make it easier for your audience to believe, buy, and bite. So instead of just telling a story or stating a point, reinforce it with facts and data. This could be done using charts, statistics, equations, formulas, diagrams, case studies, or illustrations.

Let's continue with our example of the Vice President trying to achieve a 12% increase in revenue. We can see how she could use science to reinforce her supporting argument of using LinkedIn articles to generate new leads.

She could add credibility to her supporting argument by sharing the percentage of new customer acquisitions that occur for every one hundred connections made on LinkedIn. Or she could present a case study that shows how the use of LinkedIn articles helped a similar company increase their sales. Presenting this data may add the validity the sales team needs to embrace her idea of using LinkedIn as a lead generator.

Now let me caution you that most presenters are more comfortable adding science to their messaging than they are with adding artistic elements. As a result, science is often overused and it can make a sales message or presentation too complicated for the audience to quickly understand. So be careful with how much science you use.

Remember, simplicity is the key.

Closing Arguments

After you have stated your cornerstone, shared your supporting arguments, and added both your art and science for clarity and credibility, it's time to call the audience to action. You must know what you want your audience to do after hearing your sales message or presentation.

In our example of the Vice President increasing revenue by 12%, we can see what her closing argument could be. She could say to the sales team that she will revisit the revenue numbers in 90-days to see who has generated new leads and closed more sales as a result of posting meaningful articles to LinkedIn. Her direction is clear. Use LinkedIn to generate leads and close sales over the next 90 days.

Clarity in your closing argument is the key to a successful sales message or presentation. Your supporting arguments, art, and science should have all driven the audience back to your cornerstone, so what you want the audience to do next should be easily and clearly stated.

Stay Focused on the Goal

When designing the *Basic Building Block* you need to be certain that your sales message or presentation is all about your audience. This is where you will spend most of your design time because getting this part of your sales message right is crucial. This is where you'll trim away every excess idea and only include the information that is important to your audience. Don't be guilty of falling into the trap of giving too much information.

If you want to be an exceptional communicator, you must learn to let go of what you want and only include what the audience needs to make an informed buying decision.

If you remember the audience is king, they will respect you for it.

It Works in Every Situation

The *Basic Building Block* is unique because it works in every situation, not just for sales messages and presentations. It can be practically applied to any situation, because it's a well-designed communication principle, not simply a presentation tool. Let me share a real-life example from a personal friend:

- His wife wanted to spend their 25th wedding anniversary in Hawaii.
- My friend is an avid runner.
- He likes to save money.
- He hadn't taken his wife on a vacation in 10 years.

Let's see how his wife used the *Basic Building Block* principle:

1. <u>Cornerstone</u>

Convince her husband to go to Hawaii for their anniversary.

2. <u>Supporting Arguments</u>

a. Her husband is an avid runner and there is a half marathon the same week she wants to go to the island.

b. Her friend is a travel agent and found them an all-inclusive package with luxurious accommodations at a discounted price.

c. He has two weeks of paid vacation saved up, so he will get paid while they are away and still have a week of vacation left.

3. <u>Art</u>

a. She shows him an online video of the cruise ship they will dine on.

b. She shows him the brochure for their luxurious ocean front hotel.

c. She gives him the sign-up sheet for the race, the prizes that he might win, and pictures of the route he will run.

4. <u>Science</u>

a. Gives him the travel dates and arrangement details.

b. Shows him a cost breakdown and the $1500 savings in their package.

c. This would mean a lot to her since they haven't been on vacation in 10 years and it's their 25th anniversary.

What do you think happened?

Yes, they went to Hawaii!

I've been asked if using *The Basic Building Block* in this way is a form of manipulation, and I say absolutely not. This wife knew her "audience" and she presented the information in a way that he could believe in and accept. As a result of her exceptional communication skills, he was able to make an informed buying decision, and they ended up in Hawaii like she hoped.

As a presenter, you should have the same expectation that if you deliver a message that is clear, concise, and compelling, your audience will also be able to make an informed buying decision. This is not a form of manipulation. I call it smart business strategy.

Creating a well-designed *Basic Building Block* is important to designing an effective sales message or presentation, and it's the second step in *The Ultimate Sales Messaging System*.

The ABC's of Communication Design

Step 3:

The Content Storyboard

Chapter 11

ABC's of Communication Design:
The Content Storyboard

Once you've completed a detailed *Audience Profile*, and created a well-defined *Basic Building Block*, it's time to design your *Content Storyboard*. This third step of the design process is where you will carefully organize the "scenes" or ideas of your sales message or presentation to maximize clarity and understanding for your audience. With intense focus, you'll ensure there's continuity in your message and smooth transitions between points so your audience is never lost.

 KEY POINT: When there's continuity – one "scene" or idea seamlessly leads to the next; you're giving the audience a mental GPS system that allows them to easily follow your sales message or presentation.

Step 3: The Content Storyboard

Your goal when creating the content storyboard is to present your audience with a compelling sales message or presentation that's enjoyable to listen to and easy to understand. When you include all of the content storyboard components in the design of your storyboard your audience will easily be able to follow along with you from beginning to end.

Storyboard Components

Introduction

This is one of the most important parts of your sales message or presentation, especially since the audience might be leery that your presentation is actually going to be interesting. Therefore, the introduction is your opportunity to create pattern interrupt and take them from dreading another boring presentation to getting them ready to mentally engage with you.

With pattern interrupt, you will break through tradition. You'll not be using the introduction solely as an opportunity to speak about yourself or your company. Instead, your introduction will focus on making the audience feel as if they are your highest priority from the very beginning. You'll let them know that you understand their issues or objectives and that you have a plan to address them.

This audience-focused introduction quickly establishes your credibility as the expert; so don't spend a lot of time going over your credentials. What your audience wants to know most is what you plan to do for them.

Transition #1

After a strong introduction that lets your audience know what you plan to do for them, insert a transitional phrase that takes your audience smoothly from the introduction into your first point. Remember, keep it smooth - as if you're having a conversation or telling them a story.

Point #1

This is the first supporting argument for your cornerstone. You can make a lasting impact here by being vulnerable. Sharing stories and examples that show empathy or understanding for the issues or objectives of your audience will help build your rapport with them.

Tip: Don't start your first point by reading bullet points. If you do, you will lose the audience before you really get started.

Transition #2

You must carefully consider your words as you make a smooth follow up to Point 1 and introduce Point 2.

Point #2

This is the supporting argument for your cornerstone that makes your audience believe, buy, and bite. You cannot confuse them here. You want your second point to be clear, concise, and compelling.

Transition #3

After you make the second point, you need to reference the last thing you said and use it as a smooth transition to Point 3.

Point #3

Your final point should be compelling or a challenge to the audience. You should not deliver more facts and data here. The goal of Point #3 is to set the audience up for making an informed buying decision.

Conclusion

This is a critical part of your sales message or presentation because this is where you're making a call to action. You must clearly tell the audience what you want them to do, to believe, or to think.

If you don't, you may leave your audience confused about what they should do with the information you just shared with them. That lack of direction could cost you a sales opportunity, because confused prospects rarely buy.

Creation of the Storyboard

Now that you know the components necessary to make a content storyboard, let's discuss how you structurally put them all together.

In my experience, using sticky notes is the easiest way to design your content storyboard. They allow you to write down the individual components and then place them in the order you think will work best. This process ultimately saves you design time because you can determine the best flow for your message and the best layout for your graphics before putting everything into a software application. If you need to make any changes, sticky notes allow you to make your edits quickly and efficiently - just move them around.

Creating a content storyboard ensures that the "scenes" or ideas of your sales message or presentation tell a compelling story that others want to listen to, and it's the third step of *The Ultimate Sales Messaging System*.

System Review:
The ABC's of Communication Design

Now that you have a good understanding of the individual tools in the *ABC's of Communication Design*, let's make sure you understand how they all work together:

Step 1: Audience Profile

When you created your Audience Profile, you wrote down your expected outcome, it's time to use it. What do you want your audience to think, say, or do?

Step 2: Basic Building Block

Take the expected outcome from the Audience Profile and make it *The Cornerstone* of your *Basic Building Block*. Next, complete the *Basic Building Block* by adding the details for your supporting arguments, art, and science.

Step 3: Content Storyboard

Create your *Content Storyboard* using the cornerstone, supporting arguments, art, and science from your *Basic Building Block*. Write these points onto sticky notes and use them to design the order of your message. When you're certain your message flows like a good story, put the final product into your software application.

That's the *ABC's of Communication Design*. It's systematic, logical, and all the steps work together.

The ABC's of Communication Design, are the first three steps of *The Ultimate Sales Messaging System*, and if you follow them, you'll reap the reward of designing exceptional communication that people want to listen to.

It's Time to Execute

The key, now that you've learned the tools of design, is to go from information to execution. Some of you will be able to take what you've learned and confidently execute; however, others may believe the system will work, but may need more instruction on putting it all together. If that's you, we have a plan to help.

For more detailed learning, please visit the link below and sign up for our cloud-based course, *Sales Messaging University*.* In this video-based course, I will personally lead you through all six steps of *The Ultimate Sales Messaging System*. Each step is a working session because along the way you will build your own sales message or presentation as you complete the individual exercises for each section. You will even be given an opportunity to get one-on-one coaching from a member of my team.

No more excuses, it's time to execute. So if you need further help designing your sales messages or presentations, sign up for the university today.

Now, let's learn the final three steps of *The Ultimate Sales Messaging System*, the *XYZ's of Communication Delivery*.

*http://bit.ly/SalesMsg

The XYZ's of
Communication Delivery

Step 4:

eXamine Your Content

Chapter 12

XYZ's of Communication Delivery: eXamine Your Content

Now that you understand the design tools used to create clear, concise, and compelling messaging, it's time to focus on the delivery tools of *The Ultimate Sales Messaging System*. These tools will help you deliver a powerful message that will influence your audience to believe, buy, and bite.

And just as the design tools required you to focus on the audience, the delivery tools are all about them too. This is not the time to become self-centered. You must remain intensely focused on the audience if you want to deliver exceptional communication that will help them make an informed buying decision.

Step 4: eXamine Your Content

The first tool in the *XYZ's of Communication Delivery* is Examine Your Content. The goal of this step is to make sure that everything in your message points back to one of the three steps in the design phase: The *Audience Profile*, *Basic Building Block*, or the *Content Storyboard*. If a data point cannot be linked back to one of the design steps, it's probably an add-on and may need to be eliminated.

Start examining your content by looking at your *Content Storyboard*. Talk through it as if you are actually having a sales conversation or delivering a presentation. Check for the following three things:

1. <u>Audience Profile</u>

Q: Does the sales message or presentation speak to the hearts and minds of the audience? Does it help them arrive at your expected outcome?

It's important that you look back at the information you gathered in the audience profile. Have you considered all those details in the design of your sales message or presentation? Are you clear on your allies? Do you have an effective strategy to diffuse your objectors? Have you carefully considered the best location to host your sales message or presentation? Have you invited the right people to your meeting or included them in your email communication?

Since the audience profile is a living document, it's important that you compare your original *Audience Profile* to the current status of your audience when you begin to examine your content. If anything has changed with the audience you will be delivering your sales message or presentation to, you need to review your messaging and make sure it still addresses the issues or objectives of your attendees. If adjustments are necessary, go back to the design phase and make the changes before continuing on with delivery.

You cannot get lazy here. Everything counts, so take the time to make the necessary changes. If you want your message to be exceptional, you have to put forth the effort to really know your audience and provide the information they want to hear and see.

2. <u>The Basic Building Block</u>

Q: Is your sales message or presentation clearly structured?

This is the time to go back to the foundation of your *Basic Building Block* – the cornerstone. Is your cornerstone clearly stated? Does it match the expected outcome you identified in your Audience Profile? Does the art and science – your examples, stories, facts, data points, and graphics point the audience back to your cornerstone? Do your supporting arguments accurately reflect the concerns of the audience?

Again, everything here should focus on addressing the issues or objectives of your audience. If there is anything that has been added to your sales message or presentation that doesn't bring clarity for them, remove it.

3. The Content Storyboard

Q: Does your sales message or presentation follow the same pattern as your storyboard?

You took the time in the design phase to create a *Content Storyboard* so you need to examine your content once again to make sure that the "scenes" are clear and that they seamlessly transition from one to another. The best way to know that is to talk through your completed sales message or presentation to see if it sounds clear, concise, and compelling.

Again, your goal is to make sure that your audience can clearly follow your messaging. You do not want any confusion here because confused prospects rarely buy.

You Cannot Skip the Audit

In my *private coaching sessions**, I often help clients refine their messaging by removing content that takes away from the objective of their cornerstone. I call this a systematic audit and it should never be overlooked. Since old habits die hard, be careful not to create an excellent design and then fall prey to old habits when preparing to deliver your sales message or presentation.

The *eXamining Your Content* tool is designed to prevent you from making that common mistake, and it's the fourth step in *The Ultimate Sales Messaging System.*

*http://bit.ly/BWcoach

The XYZ's of Communication Delivery

Step 5:

Your Preparation

Chapter 13

XYZ's of Communication Delivery:
Your Preparation

The *Your Preparation* step is an important phase of delivery that is often overlooked. Some presenters may depend on their slide deck to tell the story or they may believe if they have given a presentation a few times before, further preparation is unnecessary. That's a mistake. You should never think you are so proficient at presenting that you neglect to prepare every time.

Your audience is always worth the preparation and proper preparation guarantees that the audience will have the best experience possible while listening to your sales message or presentation.

Step 5: Your Preparation

In my experience, most clients don't have a clear plan for preparing to deliver their sales message or presentation. They know they should practice, but they aren't certain what they should do to properly prepare. As a result, I have created a list of preparation steps to help you deliver an impactful message.

1. Text

You should always take the time to fully write out what you are going to say. The purpose of doing this isn't for you to read your notes when presenting, that would be a horrible experience for the audience, but it's so you can get familiar with hearing all the points you want to make during your message. The more you practice reading your message aloud, the less likely you are to forget an important point when you deliver it to your audience.

Repetition is the mother of skill.

2. Tools

You must practice with the same tools you will use when you present to your audience. That means use the same laptop, remote control, software application, handouts, etc. that you will use on the day of your presentation so that you're comfortable with your setup. If you have handouts to give out or a video to play, be sure to include them in your practice sessions. Timing is everything. Don't assume that you will remember to pass out handouts or play a video at the right time.

You must practice everything.

3. Techniques

You need to recreate your speaking environment the best that you possibly can. If you will be using a slide deck, then practice speaking while clicking through the slides. If you know you will be speaking on an open stage, you should practice walking and talking as if there is an audience in front of you. What will your hands do? What about your clothing, is it non-restrictive? Will it allow you to move across the stage without a problem?

Practice with intentionality.

4. Trust

You must not stop if you make a mistake. You have to trust your ability to recover, which is much easier to do if you have been practicing your material repeatedly. What's inside of you will come out, so practice is critical to confidently recovering from a mistake or forgotten point.

Trust yourself to recover.

5. Video

Videotaping yourself is always a good practice. Video doesn't lie. It's a great opportunity for you to discover any area that needs improvement before you deliver your message to your audience.

You should listen for points that aren't clear and transitions that aren't smooth. Also, look for habits that you may have that could distract the audience from your message - using spacer words like "um" or pushing your hair out of your eyes too many times, etc.

Video does not lie.

6. Time - "How long should I practice?"

You need to continue practicing until you no longer have to "work" to present the material. It should come naturally to you.

Again, repetition is the mother of skill, so you need to repeat your message over and over until it is flowing without much effort or prompting.

If you believe everything counts, practice as if it does.

Although most clients want to skip this step, thorough preparation is a critical factor to effective delivery. You cannot neglect this step.

The priority of the *Your Preparation* step is to make sure that you're thoroughly prepared to present your material well, and it's the fifth step in *The Ultimate Sales Messaging System*.

Your Preparation:
Bonus Tips

Vocal, Emotional, and
Physical

Bonus Tips for the
Exceptional Communicator

I have included this bonus section to give you more insight on how to build rapport with your audience. Research shows that greater rapport leads to greater opportunities, so it's important that you know how to connect with the hearts and minds of your audience.

In my private coaching sessions and in our cloud-based course, *Sales Messaging University*,* I spend a considerable amount of time teaching presenters the importance of valuing preparation. The following principles, when done consistently, will take a presenter from average to exceptional.

Three Principles of Delivery:
Vocal, Emotional, & Physical

"Creating a message with an intelligent design and structure is critical, but if your carefully crafted message is not intelligently delivered, you will still fail to communicate effectively."

Since how you deliver your sales message or presentation is critical to building rapport with your audience and gaining more opportunities, you cannot afford to overlook the following delivery principles.

*http://bit.ly/SalesMsg

BONUS TIP #1

Delivery Principle #1 – VOCAL

Using your voice to engage your audience is a powerful tool, so a general rule to follow is to speak larger than life, while still maintaining a conversational tone.

The Four Mechanics of Using Voice

1. Pace: Number of words spoken per minute

120 to 180 words per minute is the average for American English. If you vary your rate of speaking, your audience will be far more engaged and your message will be more effective.

2. Pause: The uncomfortable but powerful pause

This element of speaking can be very effective when used correctly. Use the Powerful Pause when:

a. **You're making an important point** - Give your audience a few seconds to process a point you don't want them to miss.

b. **You want to wake your audience up** - Drive a few points home, and pause between them, so the audience feels their importance.

c. **You ask a thought provoking question** - Give your audience time to consider the answer. This will keep them mentally engaged in your presentation.

3.   Pitch: Where sound sits from low to high on a musical scale

You should vary your pitch throughout your presentation so your "story" is much more interesting to listen to.

4.   Volume: The power of adjusting your tone

When presenting, you should speak slightly louder than you would in normal conversation with a friend. You should always adjust your tone, according to the size of the room, audience, and microphone. Varying your voice from a whisper to a strong commanding tone draws in your audience and emphasizes the importance of your point.

 KEY POINT: You need to vary your pace, volume, pitch, emphasis, and tone. The larger the audience, the more variation is needed.

Remember: Variety thrills. Sameness kills.

BONUS TIP #2

Delivery Principle #2 - EMOTIONAL

"When dealing with people, remember you are not dealing with creatures of logic, but creatures of emotion."
-Dale Carnegie

The Three Attributes of Emotion

When I speak about emotion, I'm not talking about the emotional feelings of happiness, sadness, or anger. You probably already know how to use those to your advantage. Instead, I'm asking you to consider a few aspects of emotion that are often overlooked in traditional instruction of advanced communication skills. They are passion and energy, humor, and practice.

1. Passion and Energy

Most people avoid this very important element of communication, but you must remember that your audience consists of people, and by nature, they are emotional creatures. You need to transfer emotion to your audience by using passion and energy.

 KEY POINT: Either speak with passion and energy or just send the people an email.

Emitting passion and energy is not an easy thing to do, but if you learn to incorporate it into your sales message or presentation, it will have a positive impact on your communication.

Tips to increase your passion and energy:

1. If you're bored with your job, you should consider changing careers.

2. Add questions, quotes, humor, and stories.

3. If #2 does not work, see #1.

4. Make sure you get the proper rest, diet, and exercise.

5. Add a little theater - you already have the lights, microphone, and audience, so have some fun!

> "Effective communication is 20% what you know
> and 80% how you feel about what you know."
> -Jim Rohn

2. Humor

Light humor directed towards yourself always works best. It reveals your personality and attitude, which is great for establishing a connection with the audience. However, don't be self-deprecating, that will make your audience uncomfortable and undermine your credibility.

Caution: Avoid telling jokes or using humor surrounding a recent tragedy, layoffs, or an emergency. You should always consider the culture of your audience when choosing the humor you will use.

 KEY POINT: Using humor to make your audience laugh is awesome but using humor to also make a point is brilliant!

3. <u>Practice, practice, practice</u>

If you aren't taking time to practice your sales message or presentation, you're failing to put your audience first. You're more likely to engage your audience when your messaging is interesting and flows smoothly.

"If I am to speak for an hour, I'm ready now. But if I am to speak for 10 minutes, I need a week of preparation."

-Woodrow Wilson

The Ultimate Sales Messaging System

BONUS TIP #3

Delivery Principle #3 – PHYSICAL

When you think of the Physical Principle you may immediately think of the meeting space. But in the context of delivery, you must also consider the environment, how to maintain order, and how to handle distractions.

1. Environment

The environment plays a critical role in the success of your sales message or presentation. You want to make sure your audience is comfortable, but not too comfortable. You should make sure the room logistics are arranged in a way that is conducive to learning - proper layout, lighting, and temperature.

2. Maintaining Order

When you're presenting, it's important that you keep the room under control. You cannot let anyone distract the audience from being able to fully engage with you.

That's why it's important that you're aware of the different types of participants in your meetings, especially those who may become a distraction. I call this group, deviant participants. Recognizing their behavior early on will allow you to take control of your meeting before their actions cause any confusion or damage. The seven types of deviant participants are:

    a. Recognition Seeker - Seeks attention by boasting.

    b. Aggressor - Attacks the ideas or opinions of other attendees or the speaker.

c. Blocker - Interferes with the group process by being disagreeable.

d. Clown - Draws attention by attempting to be funny. They become a distraction to the room.

e. Dominator - Monopolizes the time and tries to show superiority.

f. Egghead - Acts like he or she knows everything.

g. Special Pleader - Introduces and avidly supports irrelevant information.

You must address the behavior of deviant participants right away or they will take over your meeting. Politely, but firmly, let them know what you will or will not discuss and then take control.

If you find it necessary to redirect someone, offer to write their question or issue on a white board and tell them you'll gladly discuss it further after you have completed your sales message or presentation.

3. Distractions

There is no perfect meeting, so you are bound to have distractions at some point. Deciding in advance how you might handle possible distractions is the best thing you can do. Here are some examples of distractions that may occur and a proper reaction:

a. Distraction #1 - Two attendees argue over a point
Proper Reaction:
If their point is related to the topic, you can tell them you're willing to discuss their points further during the break, but for the sake of the meeting, you must proceed.

b. Distraction #2 - Too many points that are off-topic

Proper Reaction:
After affirming the attendee, politely, but firmly, refocus the audience by moving on to the next point.

c. Distraction #3 - Loud noises or a power outage occurs

Proper reaction:
Calmly ask for the facilities or maintenance personnel.

d. Distraction #4 - The smoke alarm goes off

Proper reaction:
Get out of the building!

It's your job to lead the audience in the material, discussions, distractions, and unexpected scenarios, so you cannot be afraid to lead here. If you're quick on your feet, some distractions could offer an opportunity to add humor.

 KEY POINT: You should have some fun when things go wrong, the audience will love you for it.

The XYZ's of Communication Delivery

Step 6:

Zero in on Your Audience

Chapter 14

XYZ's of Communication Delivery: Zero in on Your Audience

I will say it again. Your sales messages or presentations should focus on the issues or objectives of your audience, not your product knowledge. So, the sixth, and final step in delivery is reminding you once again to *Zero in on Your Audience.*

Step 6: Zero in on Your Audience

In this final step, you need to make sure the audience will experience your best effort at communicating your message in a clear, concise, and compelling way. Therefore, you should carefully critique your sales message or presentation to make sure you're not delivering your message with poor delivery techniques that will distract your audience

If you videotaped yourself, this is the time to watch the video of your preparation and evaluate it as if you were the audience. Ask yourself, "Did I enjoy what I saw?" If not, your audience probably won't either, so you need to make any necessary changes and begin practicing again.

 KEY POINT: "Remember, it's about them, it's not about you." - Jack Welch, former CEO of GE

Things to Look for in Your Video Recording

1. Good eye contact

In American culture, frequent and sustained eye contact suggests honesty, openness, and respect.

If you had poor eye contact, then you need to:

Try maintaining eye contact using the "stick and move" technique. With this method you make eye contact with a specific person and "stick" with them for 2-3 seconds, then move to someone else. Also, don't forget to look to the back of the room.

2. Good body language

Your body language communicates a strong majority of your message, so you need to make sure it doesn't conflict with your words.

If you didn't have good body language, then you need to:

First, make sure you're not using unnatural body language because you think it is the "right" thing to do. You must be real...it works. Plus, the audience can smell a fake! You need to avoid habits that might distract your audience.

When you are authentic, it breeds comfortable, relaxed, and affirmative body language. Do you appear comfortable?

3. Enough gestures or the proper gestures

When you use gestures, and they are used properly, it adds interest to your communication.

If your gestures need improvement, then you need to:

Remember - Big room big gestures small room small gestures.

The Varying Importance of Communication Channels

People often think the words they speak will make the greatest impact, but science has found that what you do is much more important than what you say. When you are presenting, remember these enlightening scientific facts:

a. 55% of what you communicate is through your body language.

b. 38% of what you communicate is through your vocal tone.

c. 7% of what you communicate is through the actual words spoken.

This means, you cannot only rely upon what you say to convince the audience to believe in your product or service because they are also watching what you do. Consequently, you should try to present the entire communication package to them well - body language, vocal tone, and words if you want to be an exceptional communicator.

Learning to *Zero in on Your Audience* is an important design and delivery requirement that you cannot afford to ignore, and it's the sixth, and final step, in *The Ultimate Sales Messaging System.*

In Summary

You start the *ABC's of Communication Design* with the focus on the audience and you end the *XYZ's of Communication Delivery* with the focus on the audience. They are your highest priority, always. With that in mind, I have included additional bonus tips to further help you zero in on your audience.

A B Cs of Communication Design

Audience Profile:

1. Know their greatest issue or concern
2. What does success look like for them
3. What does success look like for you

Building Blocks:

1. Define your cornerstone
2. Add content derived from the cornerstone
3. Add creative art & science

Content Storyboard:

1. Creates a Big Picture of your message
2. Forces the use of transitions and proper continuity
3. Promotes understanding, retention, and action

X Y Zs of Communication Delivery

EXamine your Content for:

1. Continuity
2. Clarity
3. Emotional Connection

Your Preparation:

1. Practice using timer
2. Know your environment, equipment, time-limitations
3. Practice, Practice, Practice

Zero in on your audience:

1. All you say and do MUST benefit them.
2. Bring passion and energy!
3. Wildly vary your tone, pauses, volume, and humor

Zero in on Your Audience:
Bonus Tips

Time Management

&

Being Audience-focused

BONUS TIP #1

Be on Time – It's Important!

One of the most frustrating missteps for a presenter to make is starting a meeting late or going over the allotted time. You cannot be guilty of these violations. Not only is it unprofessional, but it also makes the audience feel like you value your own agenda more than you value their time.

Therefore, it's important that you evaluate your sales message or presentation for time killers. Getting rid of them will greatly enhance your audience's experience and keep you on time.

The Seven Most Common Reasons for Getting Behind

1. Long, meandering opening
Get to the point! Give the audience what they came for.

2. Add-ons (Remember to stick to the facts that matter)
FOCUS, FOCUS, and FOCUS - this is very difficult to control.

3. Being late
This is simply irresponsible and unprofessional, so just avoid it.

4. Lost in your logistics
Use your *Audience Profile* to stay focused on who is in the room and what they need to know.

5. <u>Not being the authority in the room</u>

The audience cannot run the meeting. You must be in control.

6. <u>Not having an "Emergency Landing Procedure"</u>

If time is short, you must know your material well enough to know what to skip and what to emphasize.

7. <u>Add-ons (Remember to stick to the facts that matter)</u>

This is worth saying again...FOCUS, FOCUS, and FOCUS.

Avoiding these missteps is possible, if you are well prepared. Filtering your sales message or presentation down to only the information your audience needs, and being certain you know your material well, will ensure that you stay on time.

BONUS TIP #2

Swing Thoughts

When I play golf, I notice most golfers take a practice swing before they actually hit the ball. It's an important moment. That practice swing is every golfer's opportunity to get their mind and body ready to hit the ball to the perfect location. They picture in their mind where they want the ball to go and then they take their full swing.

You should use the same principle when you're getting ready to deliver a sales message or presentation. What are your swing thoughts? Can you see in your mind what needs to happen for you to effectively communicate to your audience?

If your thoughts are on how great your presentation is or the depth of your knowledge, then you need to remember the importance of being audience focused vs. speaker-focused. You cannot love yourself more than you love your audience...it's the fastest way to lose your credibility and like-ability.

> "A person wrapped up in himself
> makes a pretty small package."

Unfortunately, those who are speaker-focused usually don't realize it, so here are some flags to help you determine if you have fallen into this trap.

Speaker-focused Flags

1. Perspective

Most statements are offered from your perspective, not the audience's.

2. You have heard this before

Someone told you in the past that you were self-centered, but you denied it.

3. You are the hero...again

Most of your examples include yourself looking like the hero.

4. We see you!

Photos of you, and only you, are ALL throughout the presentation.

5. Sell, sell, sell

You are constantly selling from the platform.

6. You are big. They are small.

You make the audience fell "less than" with your examples or knowledge.

7. Too much history

Your first six slides are all about yourself and your company.

If you are guilty of any of the above, chances are you will lose your audience...and unfortunately, you may also lose an opportunity. So check your swing thoughts and make sure they are audience-focused and will get you where you're trying to go.

BONUS TIP #3

Get the Right Focus

Breaking traditional communication habits is difficult because most of us have unknowingly been trained to be speaker-focused. When you're speaker-focused that means your knowledge or agenda takes over the sales message or presentation. You don't completely forget about your audience, but you may spend too much time on your credibility and talking about the features and benefits of your products or services.

Check Yourself:
Are You Speaker-focused or Audience-focused?

1. Speaker-focused:
You open with information about yourself or the company and spend far too much time on it.

Audience-focused:
You have a dramatic introduction that snatches the audience's attention and opens with how you're going to solve their issues.

2. Speaker-focused:
You use stories and examples that are familiar to you and forget the audience's need to clearly understand.

Audience-focused:
You use stories and examples that are familiar to the audience and their company culture, making them feel more connected.

3. Speaker-focused:

You talk too long and go over time. This is disrespectful to the audience and you may not be invited back.

Audience-focused:

You finish a few minutes before time is up. The audience always likes to leave early, so you unintentionally become a hero.

4. Speaker-focused:

You don't customize the sales message or presentation to speak directly to the audience's concerns, so you leave them confused about the cornerstone.

Audience-focused:

You spend time making the sales message or presentation fit the audience's needs and you make the cornerstone very clear.

Your Approach Really Does Matter

If you take the **speaker-focused approach**, you risk alienating your audience because this approach leads to:

- Information gathering
- Talking at the audience and not to the audience
- Frustration

Conversely, if you take the **audience-focused approach**, you will gain the trust and confidence of your audience because this approach leads to:

- Learning
- Understanding
- A sincere appreciation for the material and the presenter

If you apply the audience-focused approach to your communication, your audience will feel valued because you have demonstrated that you value them. This will lead to greater understanding of your sales message or presentation and make it easier for the audience to make an informed buying decision.

What is the formula for success?

The formula for success is to focus on valuing your audience's time, engaging their emotions, and addressing their issues and objectives. If you do this well, you will have an audience who will believe in you and in your product or service.

 KEY POINT: The audience is there to be served by the presenter, not to serve the presenter's ego.

Chapter 15

Using

The Ultimate Sales Messaging System

"There is a great danger in that the present day teaching could
degenerate into the accumulation of disconnected facts and
unexplained formulas, which burden the memory, without
cultivating the understanding."
- J.D. Everett, Physics Scholar, 1873

These are the words from a scholar in 1873! Can you imagine how much more difficult it is for us with all the technological advancements we have in the 21st century. Today, most presenters use software applications when they design their sales messages or presentations, and while that isn't a bad practice, the tendency for most is to create a slide deck that has everything they know about their product or service. Of course having product knowledge is important, but having an abundance of facts doesn't present a clear, concise, and compelling sales message or presentation. It's just too much information, which makes it difficult for the audience to make an informed buying decision.

Therefore, you should be mindful of designing a message that leads to understanding and avoids the traps of traditional communication methods. You can learn to do that if you consistently use *The Ultimate Sales Messaging System*.

Abandon the Traditional

Traditional communication relies solely on telling the audience what you want them to know. Basically, you lecture, they listen. This approach is very limiting in that it doesn't allow you to engage your audience in the learning experience. Conversely, with *The Ultimate Sales Messaging System*, you are taught a new perspective on communication. This approach requires you to customize the learning to specifically address the issues and objectives of the audience and to engage them throughout your sales message or presentation.

How it Works:
Traditional vs. A New Perspective

1. **Traditional:** A person knows something you don't and tells you about it.
   New Perspective:
   A person knows something you don't and discusses it with you.

2. **Traditional:** You watch someone perform a demonstration.
   New Perspective:
   You get involved and try things out during the demonstration.

3. **Traditional:** You attend lectures where an instructor presents to you.
   New Perspective:
   You attend sessions where an instructor engages with you.

4. **Traditional:** You listen to see what the company can gain.
   New Perspective:
   You listen to see what you can gain.

5. Traditional: The content has a lot of detail.
   New Perspective:
   The content is minimal and meaningful.

6. Traditional: The material is presented to the logic of the content.
   New Perspective:
   The material is presented to the logic of how you learn.

7. Traditional: You are shown how things are done.
   New Perspective:
   You get to try things for yourself as you are being guided.

8. Traditional: You attend long learning sessions.
   New Perspective:
   You attend shorter and well-paced learning sessions.

9. Traditional: You are in a formal instructional setting or meeting.
   New Perspective:
   You are in an informal and comfortable learning environment.

In traditional communication, you may limit the learning experience of the audience when you force their working memory to work too hard because you gave them too much information. It will eventually tire out. A mentally tired audience soon becomes a disengaged audience. Therefore, it is imperative to embrace the Adult Learning Principles when designing and delivering your sales messages or presentations. If you do this well, your audience will desire to stay physically and mentally engaged.

Checkpoints for the Exceptional Communicator

If you want to be an exceptional communicator, here are four points you should check during your delivery:

CHECKPOINT #1: Ensure that you are presenting effectively and that the audience is learning by:

1. Using periodic check-ins to see if they are tracking with you.
2. Asking questions back to the audience.
3. Maintaining an open dialog.

You must check in with your audience often by engaging them in dialog but also by being attentive to their level of participation. If there is little response to your questions, or they look bored or distracted, you may have a problem.

You may need to take a break or simply ask the audience if they are confused by anything you have shared so that you can clarify any misunderstanding and get them engaged again.

CHECKPOINT #2: Ensure that you are teaching well and the audience is learning by making sure your messaging has:

Purpose:

a. Explain why the information is important for them to learn.

b. Explain how it benefits them...personally.

Interactive activities:

a. Include them. People learn when they are involved.

b. Allow your audience to engage in interesting exercises.

"Spot check:"

a. You must ask questions to make sure they understand.

b. Ask someone to summarize the information covered.

Enable them to succeed without you:

a. Example: "After this session, you will be able to...."

b. Make sure they understand how to use what you share.

CHECKPOINT #3: Check in with the audience

It's important to check in with your audience at different points in your sales message or presentation. Waiting until the end is a mistake. Here are suggestions on what to do if your audience is or isn't tracking with you:

If your audience is tracking with you:

a. Great! Your messaging must be clear, concise, and compelling.

b. Move to the next point.

c. Repeat.

If your audience is not tracking with you:

a. Ask more questions to see if they understand what has been communicated.

b. Find out what is confusing them; explain your point more clearly.

c. Use examples they can relate to.

CHECKPOINT #4: Be real...Be YOU!

Humility leads to authenticity, so it's crucial that you have some level of vulnerability with your audience. If you do, you will most likely be seen as a person they can relate to and someone who is genuinely concerned about their issues or objectives.

Showing vulnerability doesn't mean you have to share deep emotional stories but it does mean that you should not present yourself as the hero in every story or example. Where appropriate, it's okay to share a personal challenge or failure with your audience to help them see that you can relate to their issues or concerns.

If you present a well designed and confidently delivered sales message or presentation, trust that the audience is pleased with you and avoid trying to be like someone else. The audience can see through tricks.

Honesty and humility are greatly respected.

"Every time you suppress some part of yourself or allow others to play you small, you are in essence ignoring the owners manual your creator gave you and destroying your own design."
-Oprah Winfrey

Authenticity is appreciated.

Chapter 16

In Conclusion

I have shared all six steps of *The Ultimate Sales Messaging System*, now it's time for you to apply it to your sales messages or presentations so you can become the exceptional communicator you desire to be.

As a professional, you understand how your products or services work and you understand what they can or cannot do. That's a great advantage. Your biggest challenge however, is making sure you don't overwhelm your audience with too many details and hinder their understanding. If you do, you will make it difficult for them to make an informed buying decision. Your knowledge cannot be the foundation of your sales message or presentation. You must keep your audience's specific issues or objectives at the forefront of all you do.

Reminders for You

As you begin to use *The Ultimate Sales Messaging System* in your sales messages or presentations, remember to:

1. <u>Know your audience and put them first:</u>
    a. What is their greatest issue or concern?
    b. What does success look like for them?
    c. What does success look like for you?

2. Decide your cornerstone and begin to build:

    a. Define your cornerstone.

    b. Add content derived from the cornerstone.

    c. Add creative art and science.

3. Create your content storyboard:

    a. You are creating a big picture of your message.

    b. Force the use of transitions and proper continuity.

    c. Be sure to promote understanding, retention, and action.

4. Examine your content carefully:

    a.   Look for continuity.

    b.   Check for clarity.

    c.   Is there an emotional connection?

5. Always prepare:

    a. Practice - use a timer.

    b. Know your environment, equipment, and time-limitations.

    c. Practice, practice, practice.

6. Remember the audience:

    a. All you say and do must benefit them.

    b. Bring passion and energy.

    c. Wildly vary your tone, pauses, volume, and humor.

As you consistently use *The Ultimate Sales Messaging System*, it will become easier for you to design and deliver clear, concise, and compelling sales messages or presentations. Not only did I use it to triple my income in one year, but many of my clients, who have consistently used *The Ultimate*

Sales Messaging System, have also experienced phenomenal growth in their teams, in their personal effectiveness, and most importantly, in their results.

What's the differentiator or the "secret sauce" for *The Ultimate Sales Messaging System*? It's our systematic design and delivery tools, which are based on how the human brain processes information.

Learning to systematically design and deliver sales messages and presentations that are centered on the issues or objectives of the audience is a concept that requires a paradigm shift for most. However, if you learn to use the tools of *The Ultimate Sales Messaging System* to design and deliver communication that is clear, concise, and compelling, you will have an audience who will confidently believe, buy, and bite.

About the Author

Brian Williams is an engineer by trade, a motivational speaker at heart, and a successful businessman who decided to merge his passions together and create *Perspectivity Consulting.*

He named the company *Perspectivity** because he wanted to change the perspective of how people viewed the skill of exceptional communication. While working as an engineer, he saw both technical and sales professionals struggle with communicating in clear, concise, and compelling ways, so he used his engineering mind to create a systematic approach that addresses the communication problems that are so common.

After leaving a successful 20-year corporate career as an engineer, Brian started Perspectivity. He has helped countless individuals and both small and large businesses refine their advanced sales and communication skills using *The Ultimate Sales Messaging System* he developed.

Brian lives in Dallas, TX, with his wife Tasha of 22 years, and his four amazing, entrepreneurial children.

*PerspectivityIntl.com

How to Contact Us

1. To sign up for our cloud-based course, *Sales Messaging University***:**

http://bit.ly/SalesMsg

2. To sign up for private coaching with a *Perspectivity* **specialist:**

http://bit.ly/BWcoach

3. For more information on how our team at *Perspectivity* **can help you, please contact us at:**

Email: info@PerspectivityIntl.com

Web: PerspectivityIntl.com

A B Cs of Communication Design

Audience Profile:

1. Know their greatest issue or concern
2. What does success look like for them
3. What does success look like for you

Building Blocks:

1. Define your cornerstone
2. Add content derived from the cornerstone
3. Add creative art & science

Content Storyboard:

1. Creates a Big Picture of your message
2. Forces the use of transitions and proper continuity
3. Promotes understanding, retention, and action

X Y Zs of Communication Delivery

E**X**amine your Content for:

1. Continuity
2. Clarity
3. Emotional Connection

Your Preparation:

1. Practice using timer
2. Know your environment, equipment, time-limitations
3. Practice, Practice, Practice

Zero in on your audience:

1. All you say and do MUST benefit them.
2. Bring passion and energy!
3. Wildly vary your tone, pauses, volume, and humor

Credit Lines

30   Boorstin, Daniel J., BrainyQuote.com. Xplore Inc, 2015. Web. May 2015.

34   Chip Heath & Dan Heath, *Made to Stick* (Random House, 2008), 20.

35   Daniel T. Willingham, *Why Don't Students Like School* (Jossey-Bass, 2009), 92.

38-41   Chip Heath & Dan Heath, *Made to Stick* (Random House, 2008), 14-18.

41   Fryer, Bronwyn. "Storytelling that Moves People." Harvard Business Review June 2003. n. pag. Print.

42   Daniel T. Willingham, *Why Don't Students Like School* (Jossey-Bass, 2009), 66-67.

49   Godin, Seth. "Really Bad PowerPoint." Typepad. 29 June 2007. Web. April 2015.

49   Nancy Duarte, *"Slide:ology, The Art & Science of Creating Great Presentations,"* *(O'Reilly Media, 2008), 7.*

Made in the USA
Monee, IL
30 September 2021